NATIONAL GEOGRAPHIC

ON ASSIGNMENT

Journeying into Rain Forests

Rebecca L. Johnson

PICTURE CREDITS

Cover (background), pages 2 (right), 18–19, 24 (bottom) Joel Sartore/National Geographic Image Collection; cover (bottom left inset) ABPL Heinrich Van den Berg/Animals Animals; cover (bottom right inset), pages 1, 2 (left), 4–5 (top right), 4–5 (bottom), 6–7, 8–9, 10, 11, 22–23, 25, 26 Michael Nichols/National Geographic Image Collection; cover (back inset) Bertram Murray/Animals Animals; page 4 (top left) Bruce Davidson/Animals Animals; page 4 (middle) Carmela Leszczynski/Animals Animals; page 5 Digital Vision; page 9 National Geographic Image Collection; pages 12–13 Simon Fraser/Science Photo Library/Photo Researchers; pages 14–15, 14, 16, 17, 30 Tim Laman/National Geographic Image Collection; pages 18, 21 (top and bottom) Joel Sartore Photography; page 20 Michael Fogden/Animals Animals; page 22 (inset) Chris Hellier/Corbis; page 24 (inset) Gary Braasch/Corbis.

ARTWORK
Linda Kelen

LOCATOR GLOBES
Mapping Specialists Limited

Produced through the worldwide resources of the National Geographic Society, John M. Fahey, Jr., President and Chief Executive Officer; Gilbert M. Grosvenor, Chairman of the Board; Nina D. Hoffman, Executive Vice President and President, Books and Education Publishing Group.

PREPARED BY NATIONAL GEOGRAPHIC SCHOOL PUBLISHING
Ericka Markman, Senior Vice President and President Books and Education Publishing Group; Steve Mico, Vice President, Editorial Director; Marianne Hiland, Executive Editor; Jim Hiscott, Design Manager; Kristin Hanneman, Illustrations Manager; Matt Wascavage, Manager of Publishing Services; Sean Philpotts, Production Manager; Jane Ponton, Production Artist.

MANUFACTURING AND QUALITY MANAGEMENT
Christopher A. Liedel, Chief Financial Officer; Phillip L. Schlosser, Director; Clifton M. Brown III, Manager.

PROGRAM DEVELOPMENT
Kate Boehm Jerome

CONSULTANTS/REVIEWERS
Dr. James Shymansky, E. Desmond Lee Professor of Science Education, University of Missouri–St. Louis; Glen Phelan, science writer, Palatine, Illinois

BOOK DEVELOPMENT
Thomas Nieman, Inc.

BOOK DESIGN
Herman Adler Design

Published by the National Geographic Society
1145 17th Street N.W.
Washington, D.C. 20036-4688

ISBN: 0-7922-8447-X

Third printing May, 2007

Printed in Canada.

Mountain gorilla

Parrots in a South American rain forest

Contents

Goliath beetle

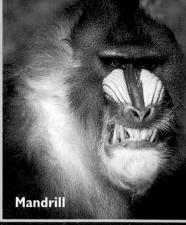

Mandrill

Rhinoceros viper

Expedition members make their
way through the rain forest.

Introduction

A Wild, Green World

A team of scientists struggles through a tangle of thorny vines. Sweat streams down their faces. Clouds of mosquitoes whine around them. Quickly, they wade across a stream. But they aren't fast enough. They step out with bloodsucking leeches stuck to their legs . . .

Does this sound fun? Probably not. But itchy, yucky, or scary as it may be, it takes an expedition like this to explore a **rain forest**.

Rain forests are the richest places for **biodiversity** on Earth. These green jungle worlds teem with life, from treetops to the forest floor. Scientists think more kinds of plants and animals live in rain forests than in all other **ecosystems** combined.

The biggest, wildest, most unspoiled rain forests in the world today lie in Africa, Southeast Asia, and South America. In this book, you'll go on assignment to each place.

Rain forests are risky places. They are full of things that bite and scratch and creep and crawl. But rain forests are also at risk. People are destroying them. To preserve them, we need to know about them. So grab some insect repellent! Get set to journey into rain forests.

Trekking through the Congo

It was just after dawn, but Mike Fay and his survey team were already on the move. Ching, ching, ching—the sound of a machete cutting a trail rang through the forest. There were other sounds, too: bird calls, the buzz of insects, a chimpanzee screech. Then came a low growl . . . a leopard? Another day on the Megatransect had begun.

Europe

Atlantic Ocean

Africa

Indian Ocean

Area of Megatransect

In the heart of Africa lies the world's second largest rain forest. It sprawls across Congo, the Central African Republic, and Gabon. Living here is an amazing collection of animals, from rare forest elephants to shy gorillas.

Mike Fay canoes across a rain forest river during his Megatransect expedition.

The people nearby depend on the forest for food. They also gather products they can sell to make a living. **Loggers** cut trees for valuable wood. Farmers clear land to plant crops. In the process, animals are killed or chased from their homes. The forest changes forever.

It is hard to balance the needs of people with the need to save the forest. But scientists are working hard to learn about the rain forests before they are changed forever.

Ecologist J. Michael Fay decided to try to save this forest by walking through a large part of it. He would gather information. He took a writer and a photographer from the National Geographic Society. Native guides made up the rest of the group. These guides knew parts of the forest better than anyone on Earth.

Mike called his expedition *Megatransect*. On September 20, 1999, Mike set out from Bomassa, Congo. His final destination was the coast of Gabon, hundreds of kilometers away.

Life in the Forest

For the next 455 days, Mike and his team traveled through the forest. Sometimes they paddled down rivers in dugout canoes. But most of the time, they walked.

When they could, they followed elephant trails. Sometimes a trail led through a swamp. The team had no choice but to wade into murky water where leeches lurked. Sometimes there was no trail. Then the team had to hack one out. They cut through the **undergrowth** with a **machete.**

How did the team keep from getting lost? They used maps, compasses, and a GPS. A GPS lets you pinpoint your exact location on Earth.

Did you ever wonder

Did you ever wonder how to dress for the jungle? Mike Fay mostly wore river sandals and shorts. He rinsed out the shorts at night. He wore them again the next day. And the next, and the next, and the next . . .

Mike recorded all he saw and heard. He jotted notes in yellow waterproof notebooks. He wrote down details about trees, flowers, and fruit. He recorded seeing butterflies, leopard tracks, and old chimpanzee nests. He even wrote about elephant droppings.

With a video camera, Mike filmed the team walking among the trees and slogging through swamps.

He recorded sounds, too. He captured everything from a gorilla's grunts to the songs tree frogs sing at night.

Michael Nichols, the National Geographic photographer with Mike Fay, took lots of pictures. In fact, he shot 2,000 rolls of film on the **trek!**

Mike Fay used a video camera to record everything he thought was important on the trek.

Mike Fay's watch, waterproof notebook, and GPS

Forest Dwellers, Large and Small

Every day brought new discoveries. The team met all sorts of animals. Snakes slithered across the path. Chimpanzees shrieked from the treetops. Huge gorillas stared.

One night the team sat around the campfire eating dinner. Suddenly, an elephant came crashing through the forest. It ran right through camp! Fortunately, no one was hurt. It was a hair-raising end to another day in the jungle.

Elephants can be dangerous. But some tiny animals posed a greater threat. Mosquitoes, biting flies, and ticks were constant companions. Some insects carry diseases. People can get **malaria,** for instance, from the bite of certain mosquitoes.

Team members had to be careful where they stood. They watched out for elephant droppings. The droppings were full of tiny worms. The worms would crawl onto a person's feet. Then they'd dig under the skin and cause painful blisters.

With a big splash, an elephant charges across a forest stream.

Mike Fay outfits his team with river sandals.

Cool Fix! Feet can take a beating in the rain forest. National Geographic writer David Quammen wore river sandals most of the time. Unlike boots, sandals dry quickly. But they don't protect feet from stones and thorns. To keep his feet from being cut, David wrapped them with duct tape each morning. The tough tape stayed in place all day, even in streams.

Threats to the Forest

The team saw and recorded amazing things on their journey. They traveled through parts of the African forest no one had ever explored before.

On their trek, they also saw death many times. Forest elephants had been slaughtered for their tusks. Other animals, from monkeys to birds, had been killed. People killed them to supply city people with "wild meat." And the team met loggers. Some were cutting down trees in national parks.

Will the Megatransect help this African forest? That question would have to wait to be answered until Mike emerged from the forest. It was December 2000. The team had covered about 1930 kilometers (1200 miles) on the trek.

Soon Mike began organizing his notes, tapes, and films. These **data** will help him make a "picture" of the forest. Mike hopes the picture will be a powerful tool. He will use it to help preserve this African rain forest.

There are more types of plants and animals in the rain forest than anywhere else on Earth.

Borneo's Forest Orangutans

An orangutan grabs some fruit high in the treetops.

Cheryl Knott

Cheryl hurries through the forest. She tries not to trip over vines and tree roots. But her eyes never leave the furry animal moving through the branches above. She's been following this orangutan for months.

Pacific Ocean

Indian Ocean

Borneo

Head east from Africa, across the Indian Ocean, to Southeast Asia. There you'll find the scattered islands of Indonesia. One of these islands is Borneo.

The steep mountains of Borneo are covered with dense rain forest. It's a forest that scientist Cheryl Knott is getting to know very well. Cheryl studies **orangutans.** She studies the link between these great apes and the forests in which they live.

Cheryl works in one small section of the forest. She wants to learn all about that area—and the orangutans in it. Cheryl and her team of assistants track the big apes from dawn to dusk.

Keeping an Eye on the Action

How does Cheryl study orangutans? When the apes travel through trees in search of food, Cheryl follows them on the ground below. When they stop, she stops. Then she sits down to watch what they do.

Cheryl notes how the apes twist leafy branches into nests where they sleep at night. She studies how mothers take care of babies. She watches how males act when they meet each other. And she observes what and how much orangutans eat.

Cheryl has learned a lot by observing orangutans so carefully. She sees how much they depend on the plants in their home. All they need comes from the trees and other plants around them. As long as the forest is healthy, the apes will be healthy, too.

Sadly, **deforestation** threatens this rain forest. Deforestation occurs when people cut or burn down trees. They do this to clear land for growing crops and raising livestock. But as the forest shrinks, so does the number of orangutans.

Cheryl hopes that her work will help people understand the forest in new ways. If the orangutans are going to survive, so must their forest home.

Cheryl maps orangutan paths in the Borneo rain forest.

Mother and baby orangutan

Bolivia's Wild Madidi

One night, on an expedition in a South American rain forest, photographer Joel Sartore touched a beautiful moth. Then he wiped his face. For the next few hours, his face and fingers felt as if they were on fire. The moth was poisonous.

Atlantic Ocean
South America
Pacific Ocean
Bolivia
Madidi National Park

Rosa Maria Ruiz

The world's largest rain forest is in South America. The forest surrounds the huge Amazon River and the smaller rivers that flow into it.

Some of the forest lies in Bolivia's Madidi (muh DEE dee) National Park. Roughly the size of New Jersey, a lot of the park is still unexplored.

Joel Sartore sets up a scaffold to photograph the highest layer of the rain forest—the canopy.

But scientists think that Madidi is one of the most biologically rich rain forests on Earth.

"What undescribed species of **flora** and **fauna** live in this lost world is anyone's guess," said Charles Munn. Charles works with the Wildlife Conservation Society. He, along with National Geographic photographer Joel Sartore, went on an expedition. This trek into Madidi was led by Rosa María Ruiz.

Rosa is an environmental activist who knows the people living here. These people depend on the forest. But mining and logging threaten their way of life. Rosa helped establish Madidi National Park. It is one way she has tried to save the forest.

Rosa's group explored the forest looking for signs of illegal logging. They also talked with local people. They tried to convince the people that preserving the forest was better than selling trees to loggers.

Call of the Wild

What is Madidi like? One team member described it as "utter wildness." Living here are rainbow-bright macaws, slow-moving sloths, and white-lipped peccaries. A peccary is a wild relative of the pig.

Danger lurks here, too. A jaguar killed one of the expedition's horses. A poisonous snake bit another. There were hordes of mosquitoes, bees, biting ants, and bloodsucking flies.

Parts of Madidi are untouched. Still, illegal logging is a problem. Loggers cut mostly **mahogany** trees. Mahogany wood can be sold to make furniture. The loggers ask people in the forest to sell the trees to them. The people usually agree. They are poor, and they need the money. But where trees are cut, the forest is harmed.

Madidi's forest faces another threat. There are plans to dam a river that flows through the park. If the dam is built, over 1600 square kilometers (618 square miles) of rain forest will flood.

Fun Facts! Many small forest animals protect themselves by being poisonous. Poison dart frogs, for example, come in vivid shades of red, orange, green, and blue. Their bright colors are a warning that they are dangerous to eat or touch.

The blue back of the poison dart frog doesn't blend in with the leaves, but it keeps the frog safe.

Taking a close-up photo of a young caiman—an animal that looks like a crocodile

Joel Sartore needed medical help after a sand fly carrying a flesh-eating parasite bit him.

Preserving the Rain Forests

Periwinkles from Madagascar are used to make cancer medicine.

Rain forests may cover as little as 2 percent of Earth's surface. Yet they are home to at least 50 percent of all living things. According to some estimates, 30 million different kinds of living things inhabit rain forests.

Studying the upper levels of the rain forest can be tricky and dangerous.

Scientists estimate that one hectare (about 2.5 acres) of rain forest is destroyed every second. That's an area about the size of two football fields. What happens when these rain forests disappear? For one thing, we lose our chance to learn what's in them.

There are good reasons to save rain forests. Many products like medicines are from rain forests. At least one quarter of the medicines used today have ingredients from rain forest plants.

Rain forest plants absorb **carbon dioxide.** Carbon dioxide is a gas that can build up in the air. When it does, it contributes to **global warming.** Saving forests can help slow global warming. This would also slow the climate changes that the warming may cause.

There's another, very different, reason to save rain forests. They are full of wonders and surprises. Without rain forests, Earth would be a far less interesting place.

Tourists to the Rescue?

How can rain forests be saved? Many people believe **ecotourism** can help. In ecotourism, people pay to visit unspoiled places like rain forests.

The idea is to "take only photographs, and leave only footprints." Visitors can enjoy a forest, but their visit doesn't damage it. The money they spend goes to protect the forest. The money also supports the people who live there.

Rosa María Ruiz talks with people living in Madidi's rain forest. She tells them that tourists would pay to see the wildlife and landscapes there. She explains that ecotourism would bring in far more money than selling trees. Once the trees are gone, the money stops, but ecotourism can keep going. And it preserves the forest in the process.

Fun Facts! One hectare (about 2.5 acres) of tropical rain forest may contain more than 600 different kinds of trees. In one study, scientists discovered more types of ants living on one rain forest tree stump than there are in all of the British Isles.

Rain forest in Bolivia

Tourists explore a rain forest in Uganda.

Improvising to Solve a Problem

Traveling through rain forests takes a lot of planning. Even with all that planning, things happen that you just don't expect. Dealing with the unexpected can be a challenge. But with a little creativity and improvising you can do just fine.

Consider the problem of feet. How do you protect your feet while slogging through the rain forest? You could wear heavy boots. But then you would be walking around in wet boots that never dry. That's not good.

Mike Fay wore open sandals through the forest. This worked for him. But David Quammen, the writer on the trek, had another idea. He decided to wrap his feet in duct tape each day before he put on his sandals. The duct tape protected his feet and also kept them dry. He didn't have to walk around in heavy, wet boots. David improvised to find a solution to his problem.

Improvising is using something you have in a completely new way. It's taking something that was made to do one thing and using it for something else. Let's take a closer look at what's involved in improvising.

Protecting your feet isn't easy in the muddy rain forest.

Step 1 Identify the Problem

Whether you're exploring in the rain forest or just in your neighborhood, things can go wrong. You've had that experience. You really need something that you don't have and can't get. When this happens, the first step is to identify the problem.

What Will I Use for Shoes?

You're swimming with your friends in a lake a mile from your house. You look back at the beach and see a dog running off with your sneaker in its mouth. By the time you get to shore, the dog is long gone, and so is one of your sneakers. Yikes! How are you going to walk home with only one sneaker? This time of year, the road is really hot, with globs of melted tar on it.

Problem It's a long walk home, and you need to protect your feet.

Step 2 Inventory Your Resources

Take stock of what materials you have on hand. What might help you solve your problem? Think of new ways to use familiar objects. Think of ways to combine objects that give them new uses. Be creative!

What Do I Have That Will Help?

You get back to the beach and sit down. Now what? You look over your pile of things. You make a mental list:

Shorts and a shirt
One sneaker
One peanut butter and jelly sandwich
A beach towel
A key to your house

You think about how you might use these things. You decide to eat the sandwich. But that doesn't help you solve your problem. Wait a minute! What if you wrap the towel around your foot? It might look pretty weird, but it would protect your foot.

Step 3 Experiment

The next step in improvising is to experiment. That means that you try out your idea. See if it works. Be ready to make changes—lots of things go through a "trial and error" period before they work.

Maybe This Will Work

You wrap the towel around your foot and start down the road. For the first few yards things are fine. But then the towel starts to unwrap and drag behind you. This isn't working. What do you do? You think. You need something to tie the towel onto your foot. You don't have any rope or string . . . but you do have a shoelace on your other sneaker.

Step 4 Implement

The last step in improvising is to implement. This is when you put what you've improvised into practice. You use it to solve your problem.

I've Got It!

You unlace the other sneaker. You tie the towel onto your foot with the shoelace. You begin walking again. It works! The towel doesn't fall off. You've used what you had in new ways to solve a problem! You've improvised.

Problem Solving on Your Own

Here's the Problem

Imagine that you are walking home from the grocery store carrying a paper bag that is full of food. You stop for a moment to tie your shoe, setting the paper bag down on the grass. When you pick the bag up again, you realize you've made a mistake. The grass was wet, and now the bottom of the paper bag is soaked. Before you go much farther, the bag breaks . . . spilling your groceries all over the ground.

You have no other bag with you and nothing in your jacket pockets. What are you going to do now?

Improvise a Solution!

Work with a small group to discuss what you might do. Use the steps below to guide your thinking.

1 Identify the Problem
2 Inventory Your Resources

Be sure to think about using your resources in new ways to improvise a solution.

Science Notebook

Fun Facts about Rain Forests

• Some rain forests are ancient. Scientists think that some of the forests in Southeast Asia have been around for 100 million years.

• Rain forests get between 160 and 400 inches (400 and 1000 cm) of rain every year. The temperature ranges from a steamy 31°C (88°F) during the day to a pleasant 22°C (72°F) at night.

• Rain forests are the original supermarkets. Some foods that come from rain forests are now widely cultivated. These include bananas, pineapples, cashews, Brazil nuts, avocados, tomatoes, and cacao. Cocoa and chocolate are made from cacao.

Web Connections

For more information about the Megatransect and the forests of the Congo region, visit www.nationalgeographic.com/congotrek.

Find out how kids can help protect rain forests at www.ran.org/kids_action.

Meet more scientists who study rain forests at www.passporttoknowledge.com/rainforest/main.html.

Rain Forest Challenge

Now that you've had a chance to become a jungle genius, try this. Pick a rain forest somewhere in the world and plan an expedition to explore it. Make a list of what you'd take with you on your journey. Share your plan with classmates. Be ready to explain why you would take the things on your list.

Animals rely on many kinds of rain forest fruits for food.

Glossary

biodiversity variety of living things in an environment

carbon dioxide gas that can trap heat in Earth's atmosphere

data facts or information

deforestation cutting or burning down trees to clear land to grow crops or raise cattle

ecologist scientist who studies the relationships between living things and their environments

ecosystem one environment and its community of living things considered as a unit. A lake, a desert, and a rain forest are each ecosystems.

ecotourism attracting tourists to visit unspoiled places like rain forests

fauna animal life

flora plant life

global warming gradual rise in the temperature of Earth's atmosphere

loggers people who cut down trees to make lumber they can sell

machete big heavy knife used to cut plants

mahogany hard brown wood used for cabinets and furniture

malaria life-threatening disease transmitted to people by mosquitoes

orangutans red-haired, long-armed apes that live in trees in Indonesia

rain forest warm, wet, dense forests found near the equator that are home to the greatest variety of living things on Earth

trek organized, difficult trip

undergrowth bushes or short trees growing under large trees in a forest

Index